BRUCE OLIVER

Destination IRELAND

Traveling Coloring Book:

Relax, Color and Take a Virtual Vacation

SensationalIreland.com

TravelingColoringBook.com Series™
http://TravelingColoringBooks.com
http://Amazon.com/author/bruceoliver

Travel Advisor & TV Host

Scent-Sational Travel & Food Resource Books™
Sensational Travel & Food Adult Coloring Books™

Axis Mundi Systems LLC dba Cruise with Bruce Enterprises

This Book Belongs to:

_____

- There are 30 pages for you to color as you take your Virtual Vacation.
- Each page has a description of where the photograph was taken to make the illustration.
- The illustration does not fill the page just in case you want to frame your masterpiece.
- You can order your next Destination Coloring Book by going to:

    http://TravelingColoringBooks.com

Bruce Oliver
Traveling Coloring Books

Copyright © 2017 by Bruce Oliver, TravelingColoringBooks.com ™
Published by Vegas New Media Publishing Co., Las Vegas, NV

All rights reserved. No part of this book may be reproduced in any form without permission in writing written for inclusion in a magazine, newspaper, or any other informational media. Proper credits required.

First edition 2017

The illustrations used throughout the book are the property of the author. Each illustration has been rendered from photographs taken by the author and turned into the line art used to color.

For more information about Bruce Oliver please visit the following websites:

http://ScratchAndSniffTravel.com
http://BruceOliverTV.com
http://SensationalIRELAND.com
http://SensationalALASKA.com
http://Amazon.com/author/bruceoliver

Printed in the United States of America.
ISBN–13: 9781970029093 (Vegas New Wave Media)

Book your next trip or cruise by going to:
http://BruceOliverTV.com
and click on the CRUISE or VACATION menu choice at the top of the page

Adare Manor Coat of Arms - Limerick, Ireland

Ashford Castle Flowers - Cong, Co. Mayo, Ireland

Ashford Castle Entrance — Cong, Co. Mayo, Ireland

Adare Manor Crests — Limerick, Ireland

South Pole (Quiet Man Village) - Annascaul, Co. Kerry, Ireland

Scene from the Ashford Castle Lodge — Cong, Co. Mayo, Ireland

Ashford Castle Pub — Cong, Co. Mayo, Ireland

Ashford Castle Breakfast— Cong, Co. Mayo, Ireland

Ashford Castle Gardens — Cong, Co. Mayo, Ireland

Ashford Castle Grounds — Cong, Co. Mayo, Ireland

Ashford Castle Lodge Horse — Cong, Co. Mayo, Ireland

Ashford Castle Bird of Prey with Bruce Oliver — Cong, Co. Mayo, Ireland

Ballygarry House Fountain — Leebrook, Tralee, Co. Kerry, Ireland

Ballynahitch Castle Stream, Recess, Connemara, Recess, Co. Galway, Ireland

Ballynahitch Castle Grounds Keeper — Recess, Connemara, Recess, Co. Galway, Ireland

Ballynahitch Castle Lake — Recess, Connemara, Recess, Co. Galway, Ireland

Bruce Oliver at the Ballynahinch Castle Entry — Recess, Connemara, Recess, Co. Galway, Ireland

Ballynahitch Castle Row Boat – Recess, Connemara, Recess, Co. Galway, Ireland

Ballynahitch Castle Cottage — Recess, Connemara, Recess, Co. Galway, Ireland

Pop Art outside of the grounds of St John's Castle — Carlingford, County Louth, Ireland

Lobster Dinner at the Delphi Lodge — Tawnyinlough, Leenane, Co. Galway, Ireland

Garvey's Department Store — Dingle, Ireland

Dingle Harbor – Dingle, Ireland

Dingle Peninsula Coast Line — County Kerry, Ireland

Dingle Peninsula Mullhaney Pottery Shop — Dingle Peninsula, Ireland

Dromoland Castle Grounds — Dromoland, Newmarket-on-Fergus, Co. Clare, Ireland

Kylemore Abbey — Connemara, County Galway, Ireland

Welcome at Ashford Castle — Cong, Co. Mayo, Ireland

Kylemore Abbey Lake View — Connemara, County Galway, Ireland

Bruce Oliveer enjoying Seafood and a Guinness at Morgans on the Wier

Thanks for your purchase

Let me know how you like these books

http://Amazon.com/author/bruceoliver

Traveling Coloring Book:

Relax, Color and Take a Virtual Vacation

TravelingColoringBook.com Series™

Purchase your next book by visiting one of the following pages. Thanks.

http://TravelingColoringBooks.com
http://Amazon.com/author/bruceoliver

Made in the USA
Monee, IL
02 December 2021